BLIPS!

THE FIRST BOOK OF VIDEO GAME FUNNIES

JOVIAL BOB STINE

ILLUSTRATIONS BY BRYAN HENDRIX

SCHOLASTIC INC.
New York Toronto London Auckland Sydney

Pac-Man © 1980 Bally/Midway Mfg. Co. Pac-Man and Pac-Man figures TM of Bally/Midway Mfg. Co. All rights reserved.

No part of this publication may be reproduced in whole or in part, or stored in a retrieval system, or transmitted in any form or by any means, electronic, mechanical, photocopying, recording, or otherwise, without written permission of the publisher. For information regarding permission, write to Scholastic Inc., 730 Broadway, New York, NY 10003.

ISBN: 0-590-32721-6

Copyright © 1983 by Robert Stine. All rights reserved. Published by Scholastic Inc.

12 11 10 9 8 7 6 5 4 3 2   6 7 8 9/8 0/9

Printed in the U.S.A.   01

PLACE QUARTER HERE

This page is provided for you video game fanatics who believe that nothing will start unless you drop a quarter in first.

INTRODUCTION

Pshoooooooooooooo! Pshoooooooooooooo!
Blam blam! Blam blamblamblam!
Kapow! Kapow! Zapzapzapzap! Blam!
Pshooooooo! Powpowpow! Zapzap!

Hey—what were you expecting in an introduction to a book of video game cartoons—*philosophy?!?*

Now, let's all congratulate these newest members of...

THE VIDEO GAMES HALL OF FAME!

REX I. SITE

REX I. SITE

Holds the record for playing Asteroids blindfolded—seven hours, six minutes. (Unfortunately, he didn't score a single point!)

HART F. HEERING

Holds the record for waiting in line—twelve hours, thirteen minutes—before realizing the arcade was closed!

DELIA CARDS

DELIA CARDS

Gave the world's most feeble excuse when asked by parents why she was going out to an arcade to play video games instead of staying home to do her homework. She said: "Reading is hard on my eyes."

CHIP BEEF

CHIP BEEF

Gave the world's *second* most feeble excuse when asked by parents why he was going out to an arcade to play video games instead of staying home to do his homework. He said: "I need some fresh air."

RED REDROBBIN

Holds the world's record for time spent standing in front of a game and searching through his pockets for a quarter—thirty-three minutes, twelve seconds. Would have searched even longer if he had survived the severe pounding administered by the people waiting in line behind him!

BOB BOBBOBBIN

Has his name on twenty-two out of twenty-three games in his local arcade. (His knife broke before he could carve it into the twenty-third.)

"MIGHTY" JOE YOUNG

"MIGHTY" JOE YOUNG

Grand Winner of the World Championship
Donkey Kong Tournament. Was later disqualified when judges noticed that his entire body is
covered with fur, he pounds his chest with his
fists, and his knuckles drag on the ground.

ANNIE JIZER

Believes she is a video game—and has convinced others that she is one.

DONNY N. MAREE

DONNY N. MAREE

Got exactly the same score in thirty-two straight games of Donkey Kong. (During thirty-third game, he finally realized machine wasn't plugged in.)

PETE N. REPETE

First person to be ejected from a game of computer baseball for getting into a fight with the umpire!

JOSH TINJESHT

Using only his mouth and fingers, can duplicate all crashes, whistles, and explosion sounds made by video games. (Unfortunately, there isn't much call for this in study hall, where he usually demonstrates his amazing talents!)

DON KEYFACE

For one perfect hour, demonstrated remarkable accuracy. Managed to destroy *every single thing* that came at him. (Unfortunately, he wasn't playing a video game at the time—he was riding his bike!)

WHEN I ENLISTED, THEY SAID THEY'D TEACH ME ELECTRICAL ENGINEERING.
I KNOW, MAN...
I SIGNED UP FOR COMPUTER PROGRAMMING.

BUT DO THEY TEACH US A TRADE? NO! ALL WE DO IS INVADE, INVADE, INVADE!
THAT'S THE ARMY FOR YOU!

VIDEO GAMES
THAT DIDN'T GO OVER

The designers thought these video games were as exciting and challenging as Asteroids or Defender. So *why* were they such flops?

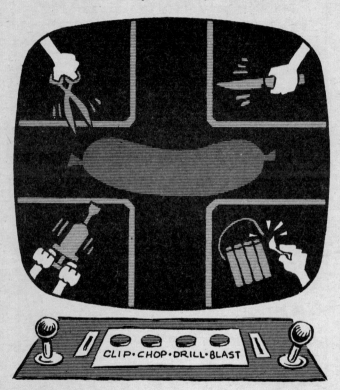

CLIP·CHOP·DRILL·BLAST

LUNCH MEAT

Game requires steady hands on the controls to remove the skin around a loaf of lunch meat. One slip and your whole sandwich could be ruined!

ALIEN HAIR STYLISTS

Aliens from outer space attempt to give earth-
ling a lousy haircut—and only *you* can stop
them! Alien barber chair moves faster as game
progresses. Watch out for razor cuts and invading blow dryers!

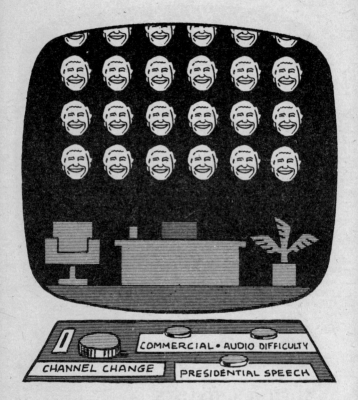

MERV GRIFFIN INVADERS

Dozens of Merv Griffins invade the earth, giggling, singing off key, and asking dumb questions. Player must quickly change channels before Merv brings out the first guest—or face being bored to death!!

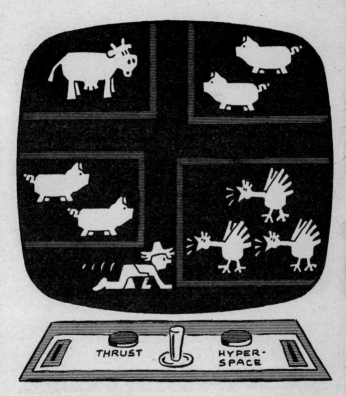

CHICKEN KONG

Can you crawl across a barnyard without being clucked at by a nosy chicken? It's not as easy as it sounds!

VIDEO GO FISH

This exciting card game is transferred to the video screen. The action is fast and furious as players discard electronically, happily shouting "Go fish!" as the cards drop across the screen.

FAMILY FEUD

Can rockets and missiles keep Richard Dawson from kissing members of your family? As Dawson's lips approach, player must blast his face—and run!

DARK, DARK NIGHT

Player must make his way across a totally black screen, not knowing when—or if—anything happens. Game grows more and more exciting as player wonders what is going on in the total darkness.

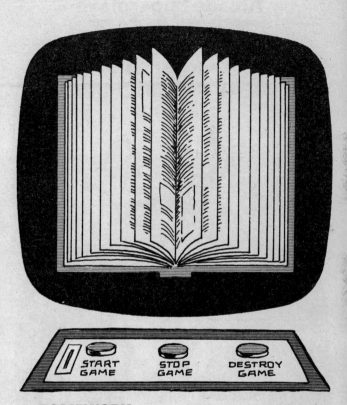

HOMEWORK

Pages of a history textbook flash across the screen. Player must memorize as much of the information as he can in order to pass a forty-minute exam. If player fails exam, he must stay at machine and reread the pages of the history textbook.

Exclusive!
Tips from a Champ!

Arcade Superplayer
BENNY R. CADE
Tells You
HOW TO
BEAT THE MACHINES

BLIPS: You've set records on many of the big arcade games, haven't you?

BENNY: Yes, it's true. I've also set soda cans, my wallet and key ring, and my elbows on some of the games. I set a lot of things on them.

BLIPS: That's not what we meant. You've set record *scores* on many games, haven't you?

BENNY: That's correct. I've scored astronomically on Defender, Asteroids, Donkey Kong, Pac-Man, and Checkers.

BLIPS: Checkers?! Checkers isn't an electronic game!

BENNY: No wonder nothing moved when I pushed those red and black buttons! I thought the machine was out of order.

BLIPS: What's your favorite arcade game?

BENNY: That one over there.

BLIPS: That's not a game—that's the soda machine. Didn't you notice that a cup drops down and soda pours into it?

BENNY: So *that's* why my shoes get all wet when I blast the cup to smithereens!

BLIPS: Come on. Seriously—what's your favorite game?

BENNY: A game called SPACE WARLORD INVADER DEFENDERS FROM THE KONG ASTEROID OF THE INTERSTELLAR DONKEY GALAXIAN UNIVERSE.

BLIPS: How do you play that game?

BENNY: You can't. After they got the title on, there was no room left for a game.

BLIPS: How did you get interested in arcade games?

BENNY: Well, I don't have a cat.

BLIPS: So?

BENNY: So, since I don't have a cat, I decided to get interested in arcade games.

BLIPS: I really don't understand.

BENNY: You see, this way I don't have to feel guilty spending so many hours at the arcade... because I'm not neglecting my cat.

BLIPS: Oh. Well. That makes perfect sense.

BENNY: Of course, my dog gets a little teed off. I feel kinda bad about that. But what can I do?

BLIPS: Let's change the subject. What's the highest score you ever got?

BENNY: I guess my highest score was 1,302.

BLIPS: What? That isn't very high.

BENNY: It is when you consider I got it on the change machine!

BLIPS: Perhaps you could give our readers some tips on how to get higher scores.

BENNY: Well, I'd advise them always to wear shoes in an arcade.

BLIPS: Why is that so important? For better balance? For more height?

BENNY: No. So when somebody accidentally steps on your foot, it won't hurt so much. I've got sensitive toes, you know, and I learned this the hard way.

BLIPS: Well, that's not exactly the kind of advice we were looking for. Let's take some specific games. Perhaps you could tell the readers of this book how to win at each game. Let's start with Pac-Man.

BENNY: My advice is to move fast, eat everything you can, and try not to get eaten.

BLIPS: *That's* your professional advice as a champ?!?

BENNY: Yes. And don't go barefoot, of course. I believe I mentioned that.

BLIPS: How about Donkey Kong?

BENNY: Jump and climb. Climb and jump. Do your best. Try to move fast. Wear shoes.

BLIPS: How about Galaxian?

BENNY: Move fast. Blast everything in sight. Try not to get blasted. Keep a sharp lookout at all times. Wear shoes.

BLIPS: Well...you're a real disappointment. I think this interview is over. Thanks a bunch.

BENNY: Anytime. Anytime. Listen—can you spare a quarter? I'm flat broke. I'll pay you back tomorrow. Hey—come back....

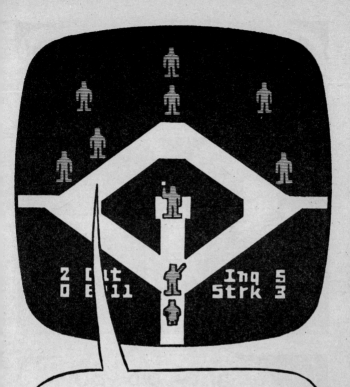

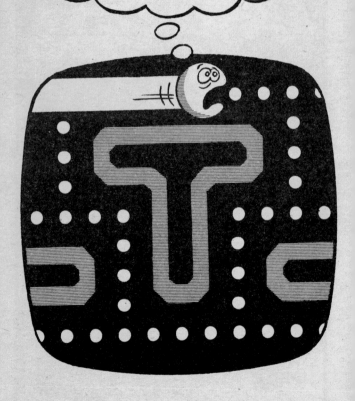

HOW TO REPAIR
YOUR HOME VIDEO GAME

Your video game has been acting sluggish and strange lately? The alien invaders have been stepping all over you? Your scores haven't been anywhere near as high as you think they should be? Well, that couldn't be *your* fault!

Perhaps your game needs a thorough cleaning. No—don't rush to the nearest repair store. You can clean your video game in the privacy of your own home quickly and easily. Just follow these simple steps....

STEP ONE: Take apart your TV set and clean each individual piece with a damp cloth.

STEP TWO: We forgot to tell you to unplug your TV first. Sorry. Please switch **STEP TWO** with **STEP ONE**.

FIG. ③

VIDEO OLD MAID GAME

STEP THREE: Remove the game cartridge from the control unit. Use a screwdriver to open the cartridge. Pull the tape out, unwind it, and wash it thoroughly with soap and water.

STEP FOUR: Remove the tiny alien invaders from the game and dust each one carefully with a damp cloth.

STEP FIVE: If your game is Pac-Man or a similar eating game, it's possible that the little yellow figure has indigestion. Reach two fingers down its throat and remove any dots, fruits, or other objects that may be causing the problem.

STEP SIX: Take apart the control unit. Throw the pieces in the washing machine and run them through a normal cleaning cycle.

FIG. (7)

Congratulations! Your video game is now clean enough to glow in the dark! You'll be ready for action as soon as you put everything back together. Unfortunately, space doesn't allow us to give instructions on how to do that. But how difficult could it be???

END

10 IMPORTANT ETIQUETTE RULES FOR VIDEO GAME ARCADES

1. Never climb over another person to get to a video game. If you can't crawl between the person's legs, wait your turn in line.

2. You will probably hear loud complaints if you attempt to tickle a player who is just about to score 20,000 points at Pac-Man.

3. Even though you mean well by giving such advice to a player as "Move faster" and "Shoot better," it will probably not be appreciated.

4. Never laugh loudly at someone's score—unless that person is much smaller than you.

5. A person who is eight feet tall, weighs four hundred pounds, has tattoos up and down his arms, and carries six feet of chain in his hand has the right to step in front of you in line without your making too big a fuss.

6. When at an arcade with a date, it is considered uncouth to carry a roll of quarters between your teeth unless your hands are also full of quarters.

7. Do not attempt to start a conversation about the weather with someone who is in his fourteenth hour of a game of Defender.

8. If, after playing a game for several hours, someone falls asleep across the machine—do not risk waking him by carrying him away from the machine. Do your best to play around him.

9. Attempting to change Monopoly money in the change machine will not get you laughs —only strange looks and disdainful groans.

10. Loud arguments should be avoided at all costs. Disputes over whose turn it is to play a machine can be settled easily and quickly by having a fistfight in the alley behind the arcade.

10 GOOD REASONS
NOT TO PLAY
VIDEO GAMES

1. Nuclear war might break out, the machine might melt, and you wouldn't be able to get your quarter back.
2.
3.
4.
5.
6.
7.
8.
9.
10.

(The author could only think of one good reason.)

It's happened to all of us at one time or another. Your parents want you to do your homework or some chores—and you want to go to the arcade and drop some quarters into Ms. Pac-Man. "Give me *one good reason* why you should go to the arcade," your mother says. Before you answer, take a look at this list. Here are some things *not* to say....

10 REASONS THAT WILL *NEVER* CONVINCE YOUR PARENTS TO LET YOU PLAY VIDEO GAMES

1. "I can't think of anything else to do."

2. "At least you'll know I won't be out wasting time."

3. "They keep me from biting my nails."

4. "Isn't competition what America is all about?"

5. "Video games are safe. I might get injured if I mow the lawn."

6. "I promise I'll stop playing as soon as my money runs out."

7. "What else can you do for a quarter these days?"

8. "It isn't as expensive as buying me a new bike, is it?"

9. "Your generation had quilting bees. Mine has video games."

10. "You may not realize it, but they are actually very educational."

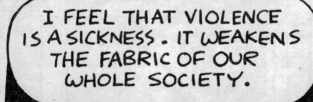

NOW, YOU CAN PLAY

WINGED INVADERS

THE FIRST VIDEO GAME IN A BOOK!
(Play as often as you like—no quarters necessary.)

INSTRUCTIONS

Vicious fruit flies from outer space are invading Earth. Their target: the apple you've been saving for an afternoon snack! You must use your trusty fly swatter to defend the earth —and your apple.

Use the buttons at the bottom of each page to move your fly swatter left or right. Use the button at the far right to swat.

Press as hard as you can on the buttons for best results. Good luck!

| MOVE LEFT | SWAT | MOVE RIGHT |

DO NOT INSERT QUARTER

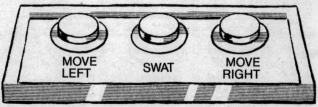

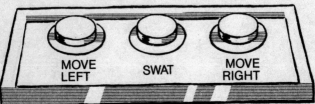

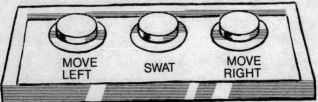